Just Wanna Quilt Notebook

Just Wanna Quilt Notebook

Record Progress, Provenance, and Copyright

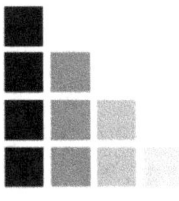

By

Elizabeth Townsend Gard

Just Wanna Quilt Publications

JUST WANNA QUILT NOTEBOOK Copyright © 2019 by Elizabeth Townsend Gard

All rights reserved.

An imprint of Limited Times Publishing House
New Orleans, LA
www.justwannaquilt.com

Just Wanna Series, Editor-in-Chief, Ricardo Gonzalez

Book design/Layout, Eyeridium, LLC.

ISBN 978-1-7341271-0-2

Library of Congress Control Number:2019916509

Please purchase a copy of the book. The proceeds support the projects at Just Wanna Quilt. If you have suggestions on how to improve them, feel free to email info@justwannaquilt.com. Our books may be purchased in bulk for guilds, shops, education and business uses.

First U.S. Edition, October 2019.

About Just Wanna Quilt

Just Wanna Quilt started as a research project at the Copyright Research Lab at Tulane University Law School by Dr. Elizabeth Townsend Gard. It is now a podcast (available on iTunes and other podcast platforms), a community (on Facebook, www.facebook.com/groups/justwannaquilt), and a publishing arm. We also are available for one-on-one coaching, lectures, and workshops. Find us at www.justwannaquilt.com. Instagram: @justwannaquilt #justwannaquilt #quiltingarmy #jwqnotebook

Thank you to Judy Walker, whose has been there every step of the way, and uses her super powers in everyday. To Julia Driscoll, Edith Gross, Stacy Harding, Lynn Rinehart, Joel Sellers, Suzy Webster, Ann Wasserman, Anne Vandermey, Jo-Anne Vandermey, Ron Gard, Sid Gard, Madison Manoushagian, Brit Staven Eddy, Susan Bunni Bodan, Judy Walker, Joyce Montanari, Meghan E. M. Jordan, Polly Mumma, Gina Olive, Celeste Poulin, Susan Perkins, Amy Reitzel, and Karen Klamczynski for taking the time to proof and comment on the draft(s).

Acknowledgements. We are grateful to our research sponsors including Jaftex, Warm Company, AccuQuilt, Havel's Sewing, the Wool Project, Michael Miller Fabrics, Quilted Twins, Allbrands, the Grace Company, Craftoptics, June Tailor, Superior Threads, and countless pattern makers, inventors, authors, scholars, and others who donated materials and their time in helping us work through copyright and quilting. And special thanks to the law students, especially Corrie Dutton, Madison Manoushagian, Chris Blexrud, Rachel Arrison, and Allison Higgins. To Tulane University for supporting the project, including through the Jill H. And Avram A. Glazer Professor of Social Entrepreneurship, the Lepage Faculty Fellowship, Paul R. Verkuil Faculty Research Fund, the Provost, Robin Forman, and the Dean of the Tulane Law School, David Meyer. Of course, to Janice Sayas, who is always magnificent.

Dedicated to the Quilting Army, who challenges me to think about copyright at all hours of the day and night. I adore y'all.

To Cheryl Sleboda, who inspires me and everyone else to be our best creative and business selves and not to settle, even when sleepy.

To Sid Gard, who has been part of this project from the beginning and long before. Thank you for sharing your creativity, time, patience, cleverness, and artistic super powers.

Table of Contents

Part 1: Introduction

Preface 1

1: How You Can Use This Book 2

2: Copyright Basics 4

Part 2: The Notebook

Name of Quilt Project:_____ 13

Name of Quilt Project:_____ 23

Name of Quilt Project:_____ 33

Name of Quilt Project:_____ 43

Name of Quilt Project:_____ 53

Name of Quilt Project:_____ 63

Name of Quilt Project:_____ 73

Name of Quilt Project:_____ 83

Part 1: Introduction

Preface

Learning About the Notebook

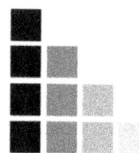

Just Wanna Quilt Notebook is designed to keep track of your work. The book is part of a larger series, *Just Wanna...* that includes **Just Wanna Create: Copyright and Fair Use for Quilters, Crafters and Artists**, which is a companion book to the notebook. In **Just Wanna Create**, we walk through all kinds of key concepts of copyright, important to a creator of every level. This Notebook grew out of that book, as we realized that we should keep track of what we are doing, copyright and provenance-wise. And if we are keeping track of that, then why not the quilting process too?

Just Wanna Quilt is a declaration, a community, a research project, a podcast, and now a series of books that help quilters, crafters and artists feel comfortable with and empowered by the laws surrounding creativity.

In my second year at Tulane Law School, I became a research assistant to my intellectual property professor, Elizabeth Townsend Gard, and we began researching the intersection between law and creativity, and more specifically the quilting world. That project grew to become a research podcast and online community. That community continues to grow as the Just Wanna Quilt Facebook group, along with the JWQ-Stealth Sewing Squad, JWQ-Inventory Quilt Project and JWQ-Gypsy Wife, JWQ's first sew along. The podcast includes 300+ interviews of quilters, industry leaders, famous quilters, designers, inventors, scholars, and so many more. The books we write reflect what we learn and what we know about various legal topics, and our desire to share that knowledge with the quilting and crafting community. I'm extremely grateful to Elizabeth who has been my teacher, mentor, boss, and friend. And now we've started Just Wanna Quilt Publications together.

-Ricardo Gonzalez
Editor-in-Chief

1: How You Can Use This Book

Key Elements to Document While You Create

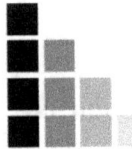
Part diary, part recordkeeping, this book helps you to keep track of your projects and your accomplishments. For instance, you can keep records to create a historical record, or to help with valuations for sales, insurance or mailing purposes. If you decide to enter a quilt into a quilt show or contest, you will have all of the information about your quilt and creative process at your fingertips. If someone believes you copied their quilt (and you didn't, of course), these records will help you establish a timeline, prove the origins of your inspiration, and document your process. If you want to commercialize your work, you will have the data to make sure the pattern is your own. And if you only want to keep track of the many projects in progress, you have a means of doing that. Here are some of the key elements to consider:

Ideas and Inspirations: From the beginning, write down where your idea came from, and what inspired the work you are doing.

The Pattern Design: Where did it come from? Who is the author and what is the title? Did you create it? Is it based on traditional blocks or a particular technique?

Thread and Batting: Documenting what you are using will help should you run out. You may also discover patterns in what products you like or dislike.

Fabric: Document the fabric any way you want. Once you cut off the selvages, you lose key information. Write it down, paste the selvages in the book, add photos, or whatever works for you. You will have this information in case you need it later. Recording your fabric aids in keeping track of designers and manufacturers you love (or not) too!

Construction: Document the techniques, tools, and methods of construction so you have that information if you want to do this pattern again. This information comes in handy if you want to enter the quilt into a show, or create your own pattern when you are done.

The Quilting: This is a second layer of copyright and art, sometimes by the same person. Again, document the quilting, the techniques, patterns, and inspiration. This will also help remind you if you like a particular design, quilter or information for shows.

Copyright Assessment: This information is becoming more important as more and more shows are asking for copyright information, more people post photographs of quilts online, and many want to sell the quilt itself or create their own patterns to sell. Do the work now, saving time in tracking down information and helping your memory. This includes recognizing who is the author, what is protected and what is not, and what underlying resources you used in creating the work.

Track Your Time and Costs: Some will keep track as part of the appraiser/worth/budget. Others don't want to do this. Totally up to you.

What happens After You Complete the Quilt: Where does the quilt go? Track it, and record label information too.

Hashtags (#) and Handles (@): When you post pictures of your amazing work, you can include hashtags (#) and handles (@) to let people know the origins and connections of the quilt/work. These are a way to identify who made the quilt, the pattern you used, the sewing machine, the tools, the fabric, the thread, the charity, whatever you like. Hashtags and handles are mostly used on Facebook, Pinterest and Instagram.

Hashtags: #justwannaquilt is an example. When you tag something with a hashtag, people can find everything with that tag! So, how do you find the tags? Go to Instagram and start to play and see what comes up. For instance, #thewarmcompany is what the batting company, Warm Company uses. Fabric designer, #tulapink uses this for Tula Pink, but there are also groups and sub-tags for her including specific # for each line of fabric.

Handles: @ is the handle of the particular person/group. Adding @justwannaquilt alerts us that you are talking about us, and we love it! So that's cool too. For the Warm Company, their handle is @thewarmco. (@warmcompany is something totally different). The handle for Tula Pink is @tulapink.

If you want to include Just Wanna Quilt, here's what we use (and we would be delighted if you include it with your photos):

> @justwannaquilt
> #justwannaquilt
> #jwqnotebook
> #quiltingarmy

2: Copyright Basics

What Every Quilter/Creator Should Know About Copyright While Creating

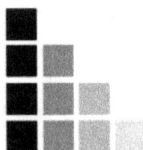
Idea: It begins with an idea. I want to buy a kit! Oh, I like that fabric. I want to make something. I need to make a baby quilt. I want to practice a technique. I love that pattern. I'm bored; I want to just sit and improve something. Where does your idea come from? Ideas are not protectable. You can get ideas from anywhere. Just make sure you are not copying the *expression* of that idea. The idea of a log cabin quilt is not protectable, but your specific version may be.

Inspiration: You start to think about how to accomplish your idea. Explore. Play. Have fun. (If you are commercializing the end product, e.g. creating a pattern, carefully document this stage, and make sure you are not copying the expression of someone else).

Automatic: Copyright arises automatically the moment you transform that idea into something fixed in a tangible medium of expression.

Creation: You will be using a whole host of resources.

- *Fabric:* Some in the public domain (e.g. solids, polka dots, etc.); some under copyright. When you purchase the fabric, you get an assumed non-exclusive license to make things with the fabric. That is why you buy it! Some fabric will have licenses that limit the use to non-commercial only.

- *Tools and Techniques:* Use whatever you want. These are not protected by copyright; some tools are protected by patents (but that only comes into play if you try to manufacture the tool without permission).

- *Non-Protectable Items:* Common blocks, shapes, fonts, layouts, stock characters, to name a few, are not protected by copyright. Old stuff published before 1924 is in the public domain. It can get more complicated (more details in *Just Wanna Create*) Go to www.justwannaquilt.com for more info.

- *Your own creations:* You took the picture you are using? Awesome! Use it!

- *Someone Else's Protectable Items:* A pattern, someone else's photograph may be protected by copyright; assume this is so if it is created after 1989. You may need to get permission, if you are going to show the quilt or commercialize it.

- *Fair use:* Hmmm...it's complicated. Fair Use might apply if you are taking bits of a work and transforming it, through criticism and commentary, yes. See? Complicated. Go to www.justwannaquilt.com for more information and read *Just Wanna Create*.

Dissemination: You've made the quilt, or the pattern, or the art work. You are ready to put your work out into the world – you post it, you sell it, or you give it away. Others may be inspired, use your techniques, make an exact copy, or take bits of your work to make something new. And so, the copyright cycle begins again.

Rights: There are two kinds of rights – economic and moral.

Economic rights give you, the creator, an exclusive right to copy, distribute, and make derivative works, among other things. They are not absolute. Sometimes others can use your work without your permission. See *Just Wanna Create*.

Moral rights are specifically for visual arts in the U.S., and protects the right of attribution and right of integrity. Right of attribution is the right to be named. Right of integrity prevents certain modifications of your art work, even after you sell it.

Note: individual state laws also come into play, and we as a society, believe right of attribution is important on all kinds of works, even if copyright law in the U.S. does not. Other countries around the world prioritize moral rights more than the United States. Right of attribution – the right to be named – is something the quilting community very much values. Naming the pattern maker and your sources are important.

Beyond law - Community and Custom: We live in a community. Play nice. Respect each other. Learn more about copyright. It's a balanced system to allow everyone to create, and if they want, participate in the commercialized side of the world. We also care about right of attribution. And we care about people's feelings—we want to encourage our community to create and support each other. We are all creators and users of culture.

A Quick Note on Kits and Patterns: When you make a kit, you do not get a new copyright on the quilt you made. You are sewing the kit of someone else's work. You are a puzzler, a sewist. If you make a pattern exactly as it appears, the end result is not a new copyrighted work. If you change a few colors that is not a new copyrighted work. (That's what the courts say).

Whether the pattern is under copyright can be more complicated. Nevertheless, you should credit the author of the pattern. You should assume and respect their copyright, unless you have done a full copyright analysis of the work (which requires more training). "Inspired by", "original pattern by", "my take on an original pattern by" are ways to express this.

And, again, we are a community. Even if some or all of the pattern is not protectable, the pattern maker has worked hard, and helped us by doing the math, and writing out the steps. Even if copyright doesn't necessarily respect that, we should give them credit as part of our creative process.

Aesthetic Non-Discrimination: Copyright doesn't judge on whether your work is "good."

Not Protectable by Copyright: Common blocks, old stuff (before 1924), ideas, fonts (unless they have things like animals on them), shapes, basic layouts, and math are not protectable by copyright. Use what you want. Techniques and styles are not protectable by copyright. Use whatever technique or styles you want. The expression of the technique (e.g. a particular book describing the technique) is protectable.

Protectable by Copyright: Selection, arrangement, and coordination: how you put together fabric, ideas, blocks, images, shapes and techniques *is* protectable. Your human creations gain copyright automatically.

Key Concepts for a Healthy Ecosystem:

First sale doctrine: You buy a pattern. You own the physical copy. You have the right to do what you want with the object, but you do not have the right to copy. You can loan it to a friend. You can't copy it and loan it to a friend. That would be copyright infringement. **Note:** First sale doctrine does not apply to digital copies, which cannot be transferred or shared unless the author specifically grants permission.

Copying: Sometimes a pattern requires you to photocopy it, like paper piecing or applique. That's awesome! There is a presumption that you are making copies for your own use. If you are copying as a market replacement for someone else, no good. In that case, you are copying a pattern *instead of purchasing it.*

Quilt Shows: When you are entering a work into a quilt show, make sure to credit: 1) the pattern maker, if any; 2) the quilter, if different from the sewist; and 3) any other resources (e.g. photographer if based on a photograph). This is called Right of Attribution. People want to be named. Otherwise it feels like you are stealing their creative work.

Commercial versus Non-Commercial Uses: If you are making a quilt for your friends or family, this is considered non-commercial, and copyright barely comes into play (unless you are making unauthorized copies of patterns for your friends). If you are making the same quilt with plans to sell the quilt itself or a pattern based on the quilt, copyright starts to matter. See why? You are using someone else's creative work for your own financial benefit.

Registering Your Work with the U.S. Copyright Office: Copyright arises automatically, once you fix an idea into something concrete. We all make copyrighted works everyday. Copyright law also distinguishes levels of protection from thin to strong. How do you get strong protection? An original work that you register with the U.S. Copyright Office. Thin protection? You take a traditional pattern, change a few things, and don't register your work. Yes, technically you have a copyright, but it's not enforceable in the courts unless you have a U.S. Copyright Registration Certificate. Not everything needs registering, but if you care about people copying your work, or you intend to protect the work through any kind of legal action (including notice and take down on social media), you should register your work.

How much does it cost? $35-55. (Sometimes you can register a bunch together for one price). You can find more information about this in our other book, *Just Wanna Create* and also at the U.S. Copyright Office, www.copyright.gov.

Why do this? It gives your copyright teeth and declares to the world you are serious. That, along with including copyright notice. We have included language in the notebook, but more information can be found within *Just Wanna Create*.

What if I don't register my work? That's ok. If infringement occurs and you want to pursue it, you may have to pay up to $800 to register the work quickly to pursue action. It's just a cost/benefit analysis.

What if I am ok with others using my work? Great! Let them know through your copyright notice. We have included language in the notebook, but much more information can be found in *Just Wanna Create*.

What if I'm just a regular quilter? You probably don't need to register! This is an economic system. So, if you are not looking to "make your name" on your quilts or profit from them, you really don't have to worry.

What about labels? Labels help identify the author, which is awesome. Copyright © is usually not included, but that is not a requirement for copyright protection as of 1989 anyway. Labels are good!

RECORD PROGRESS, PROVENANCE, AND COPYRIGHT

Part 2: The Notebook

RECORD PROGRESS, PROVENANCE, AND COPYRIGHT

Notebook No. ____

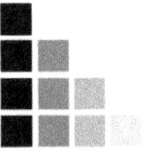

Start Date: _____

End Date: _____

RECORD PROGRESS, PROVENANCE, AND COPYRIGHT

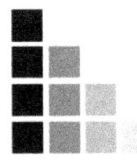

Name of Quilt Project:

Start Date: Completion Date:

Finishing Date Goal: How did you celebrate?

This will be: ☐ Gift ☐ Charity Quilt ☐ Show Quilt ☐ Commercial ☐ Keep ☐ Not sure

☐ Professional Pattern ☐ Commissioned ☐ Other _____

Recipient/Show Information:

Is this a contest/challenge or show with specific rules?

☐ Challenge ☐ Contest ☐ Sew-along/BOM ☐ Quilt show with specific requirements

☐ Charity quilt with specific requirements ☐ Other _____

Time Keeping (optional)

    Idea:

    Shopping:

    Creating the Pattern:

    Piecing/Applique/Construction:

    Quilting:

    Binding:

    Total:

RECORD PROGRESS, PROVENANCE, AND COPYRIGHT

The Idea Stage

What is your original idea? Inspiration? Thoughts?

The Shopping Stage

☐ Local Shop_____   ☐ Online _____

☐ Other _____   ☐ My Stash

What I have	What I Need

The Pattern/Design Stage

☐ Kit ☐ Pattern

    (Author/Title) _____

☐ Original Design (You are the author.)

☐ Inspired by _____

☐ Derivative work from _____

Describe the process of creating the pattern (if applicable).

Thread Log

Include the name, color, weight, and thread company for your records.

    Piecing/Appliqué:

    Quilting:

The Fabric Stage

(List, document, paste, whatever you like)

The Construction Stage

Tools/Techniques (Include special rulers, YouTube videos, books, a friend's suggestion, etc.)

The Quilting Stage

Type of Quilting: ☐ FMQ ☐ Hand ☐ Computer ☐ Tie ☐ Walking Foot ☐ QAYG

Batting Used:

Name of Quilter:

Patterns Used/Inspired by (if any):

The Binding Stage

Binding Complete? ☐ Yes ☐ No

The Label Stage

Label? ☐ Yes ☐ No

    Name of Quilt:

    Pattern/Kit Name:

    Designer:

    Piecer:

    Quilter:

    Technique Used:

    Name of Recipient:

    Story Behind the Quilt:

Description of Completed Quilt

(include right of attribution for key people including yourself as designer, original pattern maker, sewist, and/or quilter)

Completed Quilt

Type of Quilt: ☐ Traditional ☐ Art ☐ Improv ☐ Modern ☐ Other _____

Completed Size: _____ x _____

RECORD PROGRESS, PROVENANCE, AND COPYRIGHT

Appraisal

Did you get it appraised? ☐ No ☐ Yes

Appraiser:_____ Date:_____

Appraisal Value:

    Insurance:_____ Fair Market _____ Donation _____

I shared this quilt or a photograph of the quilt

☐ Online ☐ Facebook ☐ My Webpage ☐ Instagram ☐ Other _____

☐ At My Local Quilt Shop _____

☐ At My Guild_____

☐ In a Show _____

☐ In a Quilting Facebook Group _____

☐ Just Wanna Quilt Facebook Group

Just Wanna Quilt would love to see your quilts! Join our Facebook Group, become part of our Quilting Army, and share you amazing creations! www.facebook.com/group/justwannaquilt.

Hashtags on Social Media:

(Include your own hashtags, along with your sewing machine, batting used, thread, pattern, and if you would like #justwannaquilt #quiltingarmy #jwqnotebook.)

Copyright Assessment Checklist

Versions of:

☐ **Kit:** Quilt is based on a **kit** and I followed the directions. No new copyright.

☐ **Class:** Quilt is based on a **class.** I chose my own fabrics. Thin copyright on the selection arrangement and coordination of the fabrics, but likely not enforceable.

☐ **Pattern:** Quilt was made from purchased pattern. No new copyright on the pattern; thin copyright on the selection arrangement and coordination of the fabrics, but likely not enforceable.

OR

New Design/Original Patterns:

☐ **Tradition:** Quilt is based on traditional or well-known blocks, sashing, and layouts. No new copyright on the individual parts. Thin copyright on the selection arrangement and coordination of the fabrics, but likely not enforceable.

☐ **Original:** Quilt is an original work of art. Copyright protection likely. Register with the U.S. Copyright Office it for stronger protection.

    Is there an underlying work in the original work? ☐ Yes ☐ No

    If yes, what are you relying on? ☐ Fair use ☐ Permission from author

The following are items I used in my quilt:

☐ Basic fonts (not protectable) ☐ Basic shapes (not protectable)

☐ Common blocks (not protectable) ☐ Techniques (not protectable)

☐ Quotes/music/phrases (small bits) (fair use) ☐ Other

Copyright Protection/Notice for Original Patterns

☐ I want others to be able to use my original pattern free of charge
 © Year, Name. Feel free to use this pattern and share it for non-commercial purposes. If you want to commercialize it, please contact _____.
☐ I want to protect it. (Register it, of course)
 © Year, Name. All rights reserved.
☐ Other
 © Year, name. _____ [explain]

Have you registered the work with the U.S. Copyright Office?

☐ Yes. Registration Number: _____
☐ No.

Additional Notes:

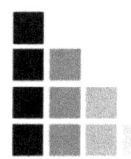

Name of Quilt Project:

Start Date: Completion Date:

Finishing Date Goal: How did you celebrate?

This will be: ☐ Gift ☐ Charity Quilt ☐ Show Quilt ☐ Commercial ☐ Keep ☐ Not sure

☐ Professional Pattern ☐ Commissioned ☐ Other _____

Recipient/Show Information:

Is this a contest/challenge or show with specific rules?

☐ Challenge ☐ Contest ☐ Sew-along/BOM ☐ Quilt Show with specific requirements

☐ Charity quilt with specific requirements ☐ Other _____

Time Keeping (optional)

    Idea:

    Shopping:

    Creating the Pattern:

    Piecing/Applique/Construction:

    Quilting:

    Binding:

    Total:

The Idea Stage

What is your original idea? Inspiration? Thoughts?

The Shopping Stage

☐ Local Shop_____ ☐ Online _____

☐ Other _____ ☐ My Stash

What I have	What I Need

The Pattern/Design Stage

☐ Kit ☐ Pattern

    (Author/Title) _____

☐ Original Design (You are the author.)

☐ Inspired by _____

☐ Derivative work from _____

Describe the process of creating the pattern (if applicable).

Thread Log

Include the name, color, weight, and thread company for your records.

    Piecing/Appliqué:

    Quilting:

The Fabric Stage

(List, document, paste, whatever you like)

The Construction Stage

Tools/Techniques (Include special rulers, YouTube videos, books, a friend's suggestion, etc.)

The Quilting Stage

Type of Quilting: ☐ FMQ ☐ Hand ☐ Computer ☐ Tie ☐ Walking Foot ☐ QAYG

Batting Used:

Name of Quilter:

Patterns Used/Inspired by (if any):

The Binding Stage

Binding Complete? ☐ Yes ☐ No

The Label Stage

Label? ☐ Yes ☐ No

    Name of Quilt:

    Pattern/Kit Name:

    Designer:

    Piecer:

    Quilter:

    Technique Used:

    Name of Recipient:

    Story Behind the Quilt:

Description of Completed Quilt

(include right of attribution for key people including yourself as designer, original pattern maker, sewist, and/or quilter)

Completed Quilt

Type of Quilt: ☐ Traditional ☐ Art ☐ Improv ☐ Modern ☐ Other_____

Completed Size: _____ x _____

Appraisal

Did you get it appraised? ☐ No ☐ Yes

Appraiser:_____ Date:_____

Appraisal Value:

    Insurance:_____ Fair Market _____ Donation _____

I shared this quilt or a photograph of the quilt

☐ Online ☐ Facebook ☐ My Webpage ☐ Instagram ☐ Other _____

☐ At My Local Quilt Shop _____

☐ At My Guild_____

☐ In a Show _____

☐ In a Quilting Facebook Group _____

☐ Just Wanna Quilt Facebook Group

Just Wanna Quilt would love to see your quilts! Join our Facebook Group, become part of our Quilting Army, and share you amazing creations! www.facebook.com/group/justwannaquilt.

Hashtags on Social Media:

(Include your own hashtags, along with your sewing machine, batting used, thread, pattern, and if you would like #justwannaquilt #quiltingarmy #jwqnotebook.)

Copyright Assessment Checklist

Versions of:

☐ **Kit:** Quilt is based on a **kit** and I followed the directions. No new copyright.

☐ **Class:** Quilt is based on a **class**. I chose my own fabrics. Thin copyright on the selection arrangement and coordination of the fabrics, but likely not enforceable.

☐ **Pattern:** Quilt was made from purchased pattern. No new copyright on the pattern; thin copyright on the selection arrangement and coordination of the fabrics, but likely not enforceable.

OR

New Design/Original Patterns:

☐ **Tradition:** Quilt is based on traditional or well-known blocks, sashing, and layouts. No new copyright on the individual parts. Thin copyright on the selection arrangement and coordination of the fabrics, but likely not enforceable.

☐ **Original:** Quilt is an original work of art. Copyright protection likely. Register with the U.S. Copyright Office it for stronger protection.

    Is there an underlying work in the original work? ☐ Yes ☐ No

    If yes, what are you relying on? ☐ Fair use ☐ Permission from author

The following are items I used in my quilt:

☐ Basic fonts (not protectable)   ☐ Basic shapes (not protectable)

☐ Common blocks (not protectable)   ☐ Techniques (not protectable)

☐ Quotes/music/phrases (small bits) (fair use)   ☐ Other

Copyright Protection/Notice for Original Patterns

☐ I want others to be able to use my original pattern free of charge
 © Year, Name. Feel free to use this pattern and share it for non-commercial purposes. If you want to commercialize it, please contact _____.
☐ I want to protect it. (Register it, of course)
 © Year, Name. All rights reserved.
☐ Other
 © Year, name. _____ [explain]

Have you registered the work with the U.S. Copyright Office?

☐ Yes. Registration Number: _____
☐ No.

Additional Notes:

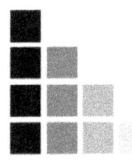

Name of Quilt Project:

Start Date: Completion Date:

Finishing Date Goal: How did you celebrate?

This will be: ☐ Gift ☐ Charity Quilt ☐ Show Quilt ☐ Commercial ☐ Keep ☐ Not sure

☐ Professional Pattern ☐ Commissioned ☐ Other _____

Recipient/Show Information:

Is this a contest/challenge or show with specific rules?

☐ Challenge ☐ Contest ☐ Sew-along/BOM ☐ Quilt Show with specific requirements

☐ Charity quilt with specific requirements ☐ Other _____

Time Keeping (optional)

    Idea:

    Shopping:

    Creating the Pattern:

    Piecing/Applique/Construction:

    Quilting:

    Binding:

    Total:

The Idea Stage

What is your original idea? Inspiration? Thoughts?

The Shopping Stage

☐ Local Shop_____ ☐ Online _____

☐ Other _____ ☐ My Stash

What I have	What I Need

The Pattern/Design Stage

☐ Kit ☐ Pattern

    (Author/Title) _____

☐ Original Design (You are the author.)

☐ Inspired by _____

☐ Derivative work from _____

Describe the process of creating the pattern (if applicable).

Thread Log

Include the name, color, weight, and thread company for your records.

　　Piecing/Appliqué:

　　Quilting:

The Fabric Stage

(List, document, paste, whatever you like)

The Construction Stage

Tools/Techniques (Include special rulers, YouTube videos, books, a friend's suggestion, etc.)

The Quilting Stage

Type of Quilting: ☐ FMQ ☐ Hand ☐ Computer ☐ Tie ☐ Walking Foot ☐ QAYG

Batting Used:

Name of Quilter:

Patterns Used/Inspired by (if any):

The Binding Stage

Binding Complete? ☐ Yes ☐ No

The Label Stage

Label? ☐ Yes ☐ No

    Name of Quilt:

    Pattern/Kit Name:

    Designer:

    Piecer:

    Quilter:

    Technique Used:

    Name of Recipient:

    Story Behind the Quilt:

Description of Completed Quilt

(include right of attribution for key people including yourself as designer, original pattern maker, sewist, and/or quilter)

Completed Quilt

Type of Quilt: ☐ Traditional ☐ Art ☐ Improv ☐ Modern ☐ Other_____

Completed Size: _____ x _____

Appraisal

Did you get it appraised? ☐ No ☐ Yes

Appraiser:_____   Date:_____

Appraisal Value:

    Insurance:_____   Fair Market _____   Donation _____

I shared this quilt or a photograph of the quilt

☐ Online ☐ Facebook ☐ My Webpage ☐ Instagram ☐ Other _____

☐ At My Local Quilt Shop _____

☐ At My Guild _____

☐ In a Show _____

☐ In a Quilting Facebook Group _____

☐ Just Wanna Quilt Facebook Group

Just Wanna Quilt would love to see your quilts! Join our Facebook Group, become part of our Quilting Army, and share you amazing creations! www.facebook.com/group/justwannaquilt.

Hashtags on Social Media:

(Include your own hashtags, along with your sewing machine, batting used, thread, pattern, and if you would like #justwannaquilt #quiltingarmy #jwqnotebook.)

Copyright Assessment Checklist

Versions of:

☐ **Kit:** Quilt is based on a **kit** and I followed the directions. No new copyright.

☐ **Class:** Quilt is based on a **class.** I chose my own fabrics. Thin copyright on the selection arrangement and coordination of the fabrics, but likely not enforceable.

☐ **Pattern:** Quilt was made from purchased pattern. No new copyright on the pattern; thin copyright on the selection arrangement and coordination of the fabrics, but likely not enforceable.

OR

New Design/Original Patterns:

☐ **Tradition:** Quilt is based on traditional or well-known blocks, sashing, and layouts. No new copyright on the individual parts. Thin copyright on the selection arrangement and coordination of the fabrics, but likely not enforceable.

☐ **Original:** Quilt is an original work of art. Copyright protection likely. Register with the U.S. Copyright Office it for stronger protection.

    Is there an underlying work in the original work?   ☐ Yes ☐ No

    If yes, what are you relying on? ☐ Fair use ☐ Permission from author

The following are items I used in my quilt:

☐ Basic fonts (not protectable)   ☐ Basic shapes (not protectable)

☐ Common blocks (not protectable)   ☐ Techniques (not protectable)

☐ Quotes/music/phrases (small bits) (fair use)   ☐ Other

Copyright Protection/Notice for Original Patterns

☐ I want others to be able to use my original pattern free of charge
   © Year, Name. Feel free to use this pattern and share it for non-commercial purposes.
    If you want to commercialize it, please contact _____.
☐ I want to protect it. (Register it, of course)
   © Year, Name. All rights reserved.
☐ Other
   © Year, name. _____ [explain]

Have you registered the work with the U.S. Copyright Office?

   ☐ Yes. Registration Number: _____
   ☐ No.

Additional Notes:

Name of Quilt Project:

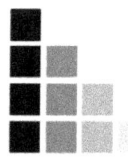

Start Date: Completion Date:

Finishing Date Goal: How did you celebrate?

This will be: ☐ Gift ☐ Charity Quilt ☐ Show Quilt ☐ Commercial ☐ Keep ☐ Not sure

☐ Professional Pattern ☐ Commissioned ☐ Other _____

Recipient/Show Information:

Is this a contest/challenge or show with specific rules?

☐ Challenge ☐ Contest ☐ Sew-along/BOM ☐ Quilt Show with specific requirements

☐ Charity quilt with specific requirements ☐ Other _____

Time Keeping (optional)

　　Idea:

　　Shopping:

　　Creating the Pattern:

　　Piecing/Applique/Construction:

　　Quilting:

　　Binding:

　　Total:

The Idea Stage

What is your original idea? Inspiration? Thoughts?

The Shopping Stage

☐ Local Shop_____ ☐ Online _____

☐ Other _____ ☐ My Stash

What I have	What I Need

The Pattern/Design Stage

☐ Kit ☐ Pattern

    (Author/Title) _____

☐ Original Design (You are the author.)

☐ Inspired by _____

☐ Derivative work from _____

Describe the process of creating the pattern (if applicable).

Thread Log

Include the name, color, weight, and thread company for your records.

    Piecing/Appliqué:

    Quilting:

The Fabric Stage

(List, document, paste, whatever you like)

The Construction Stage

Tools/Techniques (Include special rulers, YouTube videos, books, a friend's suggestion, etc.)

The Quilting Stage

Type of Quilting: ☐ FMQ ☐ Hand ☐ Computer ☐ Tie ☐ Walking Foot ☐ QAYG

Batting Used:

Name of Quilter:

Patterns Used/Inspired by (if any):

The Binding Stage

Binding Complete? ☐ Yes ☐ No

The Label Stage

Label? ☐ Yes ☐ No

    Name of Quilt:

    Pattern/Kit Name:

    Designer:

    Piecer:

    Quilter:

    Technique Used:

    Name of Recipient:

    Story Behind the Quilt:

Description of Completed Quilt

(include right of attribution for key people including yourself as designer, original pattern maker, sewist, and/or quilter)

Completed Quilt

Type of Quilt: ☐ Traditional ☐ Art ☐ Improv ☐ Modern ☐ Other_____

Completed Size: _____ x _____

Appraisal

Did you get it appraised?   ☐ No ☐ Yes

Appraiser:_____ Date:_____

Appraisal Value:

    Insurance:_____ Fair Market _____ Donation _____

I shared this quilt or a photograph of the quilt

☐ Online ☐ Facebook ☐ My Webpage ☐ Instagram ☐ Other _____

☐ At My Local Quilt Shop _____

☐ At My Guild _____

☐ In a Show _____

☐ In a Quilting Facebook Group _____

☐ Just Wanna Quilt Facebook Group

Just Wanna Quilt would love to see your quilts! Join our Facebook Group, become part of our Quilting Army, and share you amazing creations! www.facebook.com/group/justwannaquilt.

Hashtags on Social Media:

(Include your own hashtags, along with your sewing machine, batting used, thread, pattern, and if you would like #justwannaquilt #quiltingarmy #jwqnotebook.)

Copyright Assessment Checklist

Versions of:

☐ **Kit:** Quilt is based on a **kit** and I followed the directions. No new copyright.

☐ **Class:** Quilt is based on a **class.** I chose my own fabrics. Thin copyright on the selection arrangement and coordination of the fabrics, but likely not enforceable.

☐ **Pattern:** Quilt was made from purchased pattern. No new copyright on the pattern; thin copyright on the selection arrangement and coordination of the fabrics, but likely not enforceable.

OR

New Design/Original Patterns:

☐ **Tradition:** Quilt is based on traditional or well-known blocks, sashing, and layouts. No new copyright on the individual parts. Thin copyright on the selection arrangement and coordination of the fabrics, but likely not enforceable.

☐ **Original:** Quilt is an original work of art. Copyright protection likely. Register with the U.S. Copyright Office it for stronger protection.

    Is there an underlying work in the original work?   ☐ Yes ☐ No

    If yes, what are you relying on? ☐ Fair use ☐ Permission from author

The following are items I used in my quilt:

☐ Basic fonts (not protectable)   ☐ Basic shapes (not protectable)

☐ Common blocks (not protectable)   ☐ Techniques (not protectable)

☐ Quotes/music/phrases (small bits) (fair use)   ☐ Other

Copyright Protection/Notice for Original Patterns

☐ I want others to be able to use my original pattern free of charge
    © Year, Name. Feel free to use this pattern and share it for non-commercial purposes. If you want to commercialize it, please contact _____.

☐ I want to protect it. (Register it, of course)
    © Year, Name. All rights reserved.

☐ Other
    © Year, name. _____ [explain]

Have you registered the work with the U.S. Copyright Office?

☐ Yes. Registration Number: _____
☐ No.

Additional Notes:

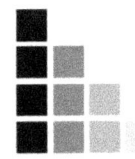

Name of Quilt Project:

Start Date: Completion Date:

Finishing Date Goal: How did you celebrate?

This will be: ☐ Gift ☐ Charity Quilt ☐ Show Quilt ☐ Commercial ☐ Keep ☐ Not sure

☐ Professional Pattern ☐ Commissioned ☐ Other _____

Recipient/Show Information:

Is this a contest/challenge or show with specific rules?

☐ Challenge ☐ Contest ☐ Sew-along/BOM ☐ Quilt Show with Specific Requirements

☐ Charity quilt with specific requirements ☐ Other _____

Time Keeping (optional)

    Idea:

    Shopping:

    Creating the Pattern:

    Piecing/Applique/Construction:

    Quilting:

    Binding:

    Total:

The Idea Stage

What is your original idea? Inspiration? Thoughts?

The Shopping Stage

☐ Local Shop_____ ☐ Online _____

☐ Other _____ ☐ My Stash

What I have	What I Need

The Pattern/Design Stage

☐ Kit ☐ Pattern

(Author/Title) _____

☐ Original Design (You are the author.)

☐ Inspired by _____

☐ Derivative work from _____

Describe the process of creating the pattern (if applicable).

Thread Log

Include the name, color, weight, and thread company for your records.

    Piecing/Appliqué:

    Quilting:

The Fabric Stage

(List, document, paste, whatever you like)

The Construction Stage

Tools/Techniques (Include special rulers, YouTube videos, books, a friend's suggestion, etc.)

The Quilting Stage

Type of Quilting: ☐ FMQ ☐ Hand ☐ Computer ☐ Tie ☐ Walking Foot ☐ QAYG

Batting Used:

Name of Quilter:

Patterns Used/Inspired by (if any):

The Binding Stage

Binding Complete? ☐ Yes ☐ No

The Label Stage

Label? ☐ Yes ☐ No

    Name of Quilt:

    Pattern/Kit Name:

    Designer:

    Piecer:

    Quilter:

    Technique Used:

    Name of Recipient:

    Story Behind the Quilt:

Description of Completed Quilt

(include right of attribution for key people including yourself as designer, original pattern maker, sewist, and/or quilter)

Completed Quilt

Type of Quilt: ☐ Traditional ☐ Art ☐ Improv ☐ Modern ☐ Other_____

Completed Size: _____ x _____

Appraisal

Did you get it appraised? ☐ No ☐ Yes

Appraiser:_____ Date:_____

Appraisal Value:

    Insurance:_____ Fair Market _____ Donation _____

I shared this quilt or a photograph of the quilt

☐ Online ☐ Facebook ☐ My Webpage ☐ Instagram ☐ Other _____

☐ At My Local Quilt Shop _____

☐ At My Guild_____

☐ In a Show _____

☐ In a Quilting Facebook Group _____

☐ Just Wanna Quilt Facebook Group

Just Wanna Quilt would love to see your quilts! Join our Facebook Group, become part of our Quilting Army, and share you amazing creations! www.facebook.com/group/justwannaquilt.

Hashtags on Social Media:

(Include your own hashtags, along with your sewing machine, batting used, thread, pattern, and if you would like #justwannaquilt #quiltingarmy #jwqnotebook.)

Copyright Assessment Checklist

Versions of:

☐ **Kit:** Quilt is based on a **kit** and I followed the directions. No new copyright.

☐ **Class:** Quilt is based on a **class.** I chose my own fabrics. Thin copyright on the selection arrangement and coordination of the fabrics, but likely not enforceable.

☐ **Pattern:** Quilt was made from purchased pattern. No new copyright on the pattern; thin copyright on the selection arrangement and coordination of the fabrics, but likely not enforceable.

OR

New Design/Original Patterns:

☐ **Tradition:** Quilt is based on traditional or well-known blocks, sashing, and layouts. No new copyright on the individual parts. Thin copyright on the selection arrangement and coordination of the fabrics, but likely not enforceable.

☐ **Original:** Quilt is an original work of art. Copyright protection likely. Register with the U.S. Copyright Office it for stronger protection.

    Is there an underlying work in the original work?   ☐ Yes ☐ No

    If yes, what are you relying on? ☐ Fair use ☐ Permission from author

The following are items I used in my quilt:

☐ Basic fonts (not protectable)   ☐ Basic shapes (not protectable)

☐ Common blocks (not protectable)   ☐ Techniques (not protectable)

☐ Quotes/music/phrases (small bits) (fair use)   ☐ Other

RECORD PROGRESS, PROVENANCE, AND COPYRIGHT

Copyright Protection/Notice for Original Patterns

☐ I want others to be able to use my original pattern free of charge
    © Year, Name. Feel free to use this pattern and share it for non-commercial purposes.
    If you want to commercialize it, please contact _____.
☐ I want to protect it. (Register it, of course)
    © Year, Name. All rights reserved.
☐ Other
    © Year, name. _____ [explain]

Have you registered the work with the U.S. Copyright Office?

    ☐ Yes. Registration Number: _____
    ☐ No.

Additional Notes:

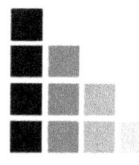

Name of Quilt Project:

Start Date: Completion Date:

Finishing Date Goal: How did you celebrate?

This will be: ☐ Gift ☐ Charity Quilt ☐ Show Quilt ☐ Commercial ☐ Keep ☐ Not sure

☐ Professional Pattern ☐ Commissioned ☐ Other _____

Recipient/Show Information:

Is this a contest/challenge or show with specific rules?

☐ Challenge ☐ Contest ☐ Sew-along/BOM ☐ Quilt Show with specific requirements

☐ Charity quilt with specific requirements ☐ Other _____

Time Keeping (optional)

    Idea:

    Shopping:

    Creating the Pattern:

    Piecing/Applique/Construction:

    Quilting:

    Binding:

    Total:

The Idea Stage

What is your original idea? Inspiration? Thoughts?

The Shopping Stage

☐ Local Shop_____ ☐ Online _____

☐ Other _____ ☐ My Stash

What I have	What I Need

The Pattern/Design Stage

☐ Kit ☐ Pattern

    (Author/Title) _____

☐ Original Design (You are the author.)

☐ Inspired by _____

☐ Derivative work from _____

Describe the process of creating the pattern (if applicable).

Thread Log

Include the name, color, weight, and thread company for your records.

    Piecing/Appliqué:

    Quilting:

The Fabric Stage

(List, document, paste, whatever you like)

The Construction Stage

Tools/Techniques (Include special rulers, YouTube videos, books, a friend's suggestion, etc.)

The Quilting Stage

Type of Quilting: ☐ FMQ ☐ Hand ☐ Computer ☐ Tie ☐ Walking Foot ☐ QAYG

Batting Used:

Name of Quilter:

Patterns Used/Inspired by (if any):

The Binding Stage

Binding Complete? ☐ Yes ☐ No

The Label Stage

Label? ☐ Yes ☐ No

    Name of Quilt:

    Pattern/Kit Name:

    Designer:

    Piecer:

    Quilter:

    Technique Used:

    Name of Recipient:

    Story Behind the Quilt:

Description of Completed Quilt

(include right of attribution for key people including yourself as designer, original pattern maker, sewist, and/or quilter)

Completed Quilt

Type of Quilt: ☐ Traditional ☐ Art ☐ Improv ☐ Modern ☐ Other_____

Completed Size: _____ x _____

Appraisal

Did you get it appraised?   ☐ No ☐ Yes

Appraiser:_____   Date:_____

Appraisal Value:

　　　　Insurance:_____　Fair Market _____ Donation _____

I shared this quilt or a photograph of the quilt

☐ Online ☐ Facebook ☐ My Webpage ☐ Instagram ☐ Other _____

☐ At My Local Quilt Shop _____

☐ At My Guild_____

☐ In a Show _____

☐ In a Quilting Facebook Group _____

☐ Just Wanna Quilt Facebook Group

Just Wanna Quilt would love to see your quilts! Join our Facebook Group, become part of our Quilting Army, and share you amazing creations! www.facebook.com/group/justwannaquilt.

Hashtags on Social Media:

(Include your own hashtags, along with your sewing machine, batting used, thread, pattern, and if you would like #justwannaquilt #quiltingarmy #jwqnotebook.)

Copyright Assessment Checklist

Versions of:

☐ **Kit:** Quilt is based on a **kit** and I followed the directions. No new copyright.

☐ **Class:** Quilt is based on a **class.** I chose my own fabrics. Thin copyright on the selection arrangement and coordination of the fabrics, but likely not enforceable.

☐ **Pattern:** Quilt was made from purchased pattern. No new copyright on the pattern; thin copyright on the selection arrangement and coordination of the fabrics, but likely not enforceable.

OR

New Design/Original Patterns:

☐ **Tradition:** Quilt is based on traditional or well-known blocks, sashing, and layouts. No new copyright on the individual parts. Thin copyright on the selection arrangement and coordination of the fabrics, but likely not enforceable.

☐ **Original:** Quilt is an original work of art. Copyright protection likely. Register with the U.S. Copyright Office it for stronger protection.

    Is there an underlying work in the original work?   ☐ Yes ☐ No

    If yes, what are you relying on? ☐ Fair use ☐ Permission from author

The following are items I used in my quilt:

☐ Basic fonts (not protectable)   ☐ Basic shapes (not protectable)

☐ Common blocks (not protectable)   ☐ Techniques (not protectable)

☐ Quotes/music/phrases (small bits) (fair use)   ☐ Other

Copyright Protection/Notice for Original Patterns

☐ I want others to be able to use my original pattern free of charge
    © Year, Name. Feel free to use this pattern and share it for non-commercial purposes. If you want to commercialize it, please contact _____.

☐ I want to protect it. (Register it, of course)
    © Year, Name. All rights reserved.

☐ Other
    © Year, name. _____ [explain]

Have you registered the work with the U.S. Copyright Office?

☐ Yes. Registration Number: _____
☐ No.

Additional Notes:

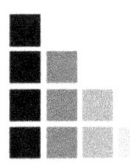

Name of Quilt Project:

Start Date: Completion Date:

Finishing Date Goal: How did you celebrate?

This will be: ☐ Gift ☐ Charity Quilt ☐ Show Quilt ☐ Commercial ☐ Keep ☐ Not sure

☐ Professional Pattern ☐ Commissioned ☐ Other _____

Recipient/Show Information:

Is this a contest/challenge or show with specific rules?

☐ Challenge ☐ Contest ☐ Sew-along/BOM ☐ Quilt Show with specific requirements

☐ Charity quilt with specific requirements ☐ Other _____

Time Keeping (optional)

    Idea:

    Shopping:

    Creating the Pattern:

    Piecing/Applique/Construction:

    Quilting:

    Binding:

    Total:

The Idea Stage

What is your original idea? Inspiration? Thoughts?

The Shopping Stage

☐ Local Shop_____ ☐ Online _____

☐ Other _____ ☐ My Stash

What I have	What I Need

The Pattern/Design Stage

☐ Kit ☐ Pattern

    (Author/Title) _____

☐ Original Design (You are the author.)

☐ Inspired by _____

☐ Derivative work from _____

Describe the process of creating the pattern (if applicable).

Thread Log

Include the name, color, weight, and thread company for your records.

    Piecing/Appliqué:

    Quilting:

The Fabric Stage

(List, document, paste, whatever you like)

The Construction Stage

Tools/Techniques (Include special rulers, YouTube videos, books, a friend's suggestion, etc.)

The Quilting Stage

Type of Quilting: ☐ FMQ ☐ Hand ☐ Computer ☐ Tie ☐ Walking Foot ☐ QAYG

Batting Used:

Name of Quilter:

Patterns Used/Inspired by (if any):

The Binding Stage

Binding Complete? ☐ Yes ☐ No

The Label Stage

Label? ☐ Yes ☐ No

    Name of Quilt:

    Pattern/Kit Name:

    Designer:

    Piecer:

    Quilter:

    Technique Used:

    Name of Recipient:

    Story Behind the Quilt:

Description of Completed Quilt

(include right of attribution for key people including yourself as designer, original pattern maker, sewist, and/or quilter)

Completed Quilt

Type of Quilt: ☐ Traditional ☐ Art ☐ Improv ☐ Modern ☐ Other _____

Completed Size: _____ x _____

Appraisal

Did you get it appraised? ☐ No ☐ Yes

Appraiser:_____   Date:_____

Appraisal Value:

     Insurance:_____   Fair Market _____   Donation _____

I shared this quilt or a photograph of the quilt

☐ Online ☐ Facebook ☐ My Webpage ☐ Instagram ☐ Other _____

☐ At My Local Quilt Shop _____

☐ At My Guild _____

☐ In a Show _____

☐ In a Quilting Facebook Group _____

☐ Just Wanna Quilt Facebook Group

Just Wanna Quilt would love to see your quilts! Join our Facebook Group, become part of our Quilting Army, and share you amazing creations! www.facebook.com/group/justwannaquilt.

Hashtags on Social Media:

(Include your own hashtags, along with your sewing machine, batting used, thread, pattern, and if you would like #justwannaquilt #quiltingarmy #jwqnotebook.)

Copyright Assessment Checklist

Versions of:

☐ **Kit:** Quilt is based on a **kit** and I followed the directions. No new copyright.

☐ **Class:** Quilt is based on a **class.** I chose my own fabrics. Thin copyright on the selection arrangement and coordination of the fabrics, but likely not enforceable.

☐ **Pattern:** Quilt was made from purchased pattern. No new copyright on the pattern; thin copyright on the selection arrangement and coordination of the fabrics, but likely not enforceable.

OR

New Design/Original Patterns:

☐ **Tradition:** Quilt is based on traditional or well-known blocks, sashing, and layouts. No new copyright on the individual parts. Thin copyright on the selection arrangement and coordination of the fabrics, but likely not enforceable.

☐ **Original:** Quilt is an original work of art. Copyright protection likely. Register with the U.S. Copyright Office it for stronger protection.

    Is there an underlying work in the original work?　☐ Yes ☐ No

    If yes, what are you relying on? ☐ Fair use ☐ Permission from author

The following are items I used in my quilt:

☐ Basic fonts (not protectable)　　　　　☐ Basic shapes (not protectable)

☐ Common blocks (not protectable)　　　☐ Techniques (not protectable)

☐ Quotes/music/phrases (small bits) (fair use)　　☐ Other

Copyright Protection/Notice for Original Patterns

☐ I want others to be able to use my original pattern free of charge
    © Year, Name. Feel free to use this pattern and share it for non-commercial purposes.
     If you want to commercialize it, please contact _____.
☐ I want to protect it. (Register it, of course)
    © Year, Name. All rights reserved.
☐ Other
    © Year, name. _____ [explain]

Have you registered the work with the U.S. Copyright Office?

    ☐ Yes. Registration Number: _____
    ☐ No.

Additional Notes:

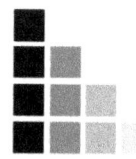

Name of Quilt Project:

Start Date: Completion Date:

Finishing Date Goal: How did you celebrate?

This will be: ☐ Gift ☐ Charity Quilt ☐ Show Quilt ☐ Commercial ☐ Keep ☐ Not sure

☐ Professional Pattern ☐ Commissioned ☐ Other _____

Recipient/Show Information:

Is this a contest/challenge or show with specific rules?

☐ Challenge ☐ Contest ☐ Sew-along/BOM ☐ Quilt Show with specific requirements

☐ Charity quilt with specific requirements ☐ Other _____

Time Keeping (optional)

    Idea:

    Shopping:

    Creating the Pattern:

    Piecing/Applique/Construction:

    Quilting:

    Binding:

    Total:

The Idea Stage

What is your original idea? Inspiration? Thoughts?

The Shopping Stage

☐ Local Shop_____ ☐ Online _____

☐ Other _____ ☐ My Stash

What I have	What I Need

RECORD PROGRESS, PROVENANCE, AND COPYRIGHT

The Pattern/Design Stage

☐ Kit ☐ Pattern

    (Author/Title) _____

☐ Original Design (You are the author.)

☐ Inspired by _____

☐ Derivative work from _____

Describe the process of creating the pattern (if applicable).

Thread Log

Include the name, color, weight, and thread company for your records.

    Piecing/Appliqué:

    Quilting:

The Fabric Stage

(List, document, paste, whatever you like)

The Construction Stage

Tools/Techniques (Include special rulers, YouTube videos, books, a friend's suggestion, etc.)

The Quilting Stage

Type of Quilting: ☐ FMQ ☐ Hand ☐ Computer ☐ Tie ☐ Walking Foot ☐ QAYG

Batting Used:

Name of Quilter:

Patterns Used/Inspired by (if any):

The Binding Stage

Binding Complete? ☐ Yes ☐ No

The Label Stage

Label? ☐ Yes ☐ No

    Name of Quilt:

    Pattern/Kit Name:

    Designer:

    Piecer:

    Quilter:

    Technique Used:

    Name of Recipient:

    Story Behind the Quilt:

Description of Completed Quilt

(include right of attribution for key people including yourself as designer, original pattern maker, sewist, and/or quilter)

Completed Quilt

Type of Quilt: ☐ Traditional ☐ Art ☐ Improv ☐ Modern ☐ Other _____

Completed Size: _____ x _____

RECORD PROGRESS, PROVENANCE, AND COPYRIGHT

Appraisal

Did you get it appraised? ☐ No ☐ Yes

Appraiser:_____ Date:_____

Appraisal Value:

      Insurance:_____ Fair Market _____ Donation _____

I shared this quilt or a photograph of the quilt

☐ Online ☐ Facebook ☐ My Webpage ☐ Instagram ☐ Other _____

☐ At My Local Quilt Shop _____

☐ At My Guild_____

☐ In a Show _____

☐ In a Quilting Facebook Group _____

☐ Just Wanna Quilt Facebook Group

Just Wanna Quilt would love to see your quilts! Join our Facebook Group, become part of our Quilting Army, and share you amazing creations! www.facebook.com/group/justwannaquilt.

Hashtags on Social Media:

(Include your own hashtags, along with your sewing machine, batting used, thread, pattern, and if you would like #justwannaquilt #quiltingarmy #jwqnotebook.)

Copyright Assessment Checklist

Versions of:

☐ **Kit:** Quilt is based on a **kit** and I followed the directions. No new copyright.

☐ **Class:** Quilt is based on a **class**. I chose my own fabrics. Thin copyright on the selection arrangement and coordination of the fabrics, but likely not enforceable.

☐ **Pattern:** Quilt was made from purchased pattern. No new copyright on the pattern; thin copyright on the selection arrangement and coordination of the fabrics, but likely not enforceable.

OR

New Design/Original Patterns:

☐ **Tradition:** Quilt is based on traditional or well-known blocks, sashing, and layouts. No new copyright on the individual parts. Thin copyright on the selection arrangement and coordination of the fabrics, but likely not enforceable.

☐ **Original:** Quilt is an original work of art. Copyright protection likely. Register with the U.S. Copyright Office it for stronger protection.

    Is there an underlying work in the original work? ☐ Yes ☐ No

    If yes, what are you relying on? ☐ Fair use ☐ Permission from author

The following are items I used in my quilt:

☐ Basic fonts (not protectable) ☐ Basic shapes (not protectable)

☐ Common blocks (not protectable) ☐ Techniques (not protectable)

☐ Quotes/music/phrases (small bits) (fair use) ☐ Other

Copyright Protection/Notice for Original Patterns

☐ I want others to be able to use my original pattern free of charge
    © Year, Name. Feel free to use this pattern and share it for non-commercial purposes.
    If you want to commercialize it, please contact _____.

☐ I want to protect it. (Register it, of course)
    © Year, Name. All rights reserved.

☐ Other
    © Year, name. _____ [explain]

Have you registered the work with the U.S. Copyright Office?

☐ Yes. Registration Number: _____
☐ No.

Additional Notes:

www.ingramcontent.com/pod-product-compliance
Lightning Source LLC
Chambersburg PA
CBHW051353070526

44584CB00025B/3750